FAITH
IN ACTION

The Transformative Power of Trusting God's Plan

RICHARD D. HOWELL, JR.

FAITH IN ACTION © copyright 2017 by Richard D. Howell, Jr. All rights reserved. No part of this book may be reproduced in any form whatsoever, by photography or xerography or by any other means, by broadcast or transmission, by translation into any kind of language, nor by recording electronically or otherwise, without permission in writing from the author, except by a reviewer, who may quote brief passages in critical articles or reviews.

ISBN: 978-1-945769-15-3
Library of Congress Catalog Number: 2016953452

Printed in the United States of America
First Printing: 2016
20   19   18   17   16   5   4   3   2   1

Cover Design by Nupoor Gordon

Wise Ink Creative Publishing
837 Glenwood Ave.
Minneapolis, MN 55405
www.wiseinkpub.com

*I dedicate this book to the memory of
my dad, Richard Sr., whose faith in God
led him home to glory this year.*

CONTENTS

Introduction	7
The Faith Myths	15
Faith: God's Perfect Plan in a Messed-Up World	30
The Faith of Jesus	40
Faith: The Power in Us	52
The God Wars	61
The Transformational Power of Faith	73
Faith-in-Action Prayers	80
Faith-in-Action Stories	86
Acknowledgments	102
About Bishop Richard D. Howell, Jr.	103

INTRODUCTION

He replied, "Because you have so little faith. Truly I tell you, if you have faith as small as a mustard seed, you can say to this mountain, 'Move from here to there,' and it will move. Nothing will be impossible for you."

—MATTHEW 17:20

What does it mean to have an authentic relationship with something that is invisible? As a pastor, I've often reflected about how as Christians we're charged to place our faith in what we frequently can neither see nor touch. As life throws us curve balls, and as setbacks pull us into murky waters, "have faith" is the advice we're given time and again. But, let's be honest, it's tough to have faith, especially in our darkest moments. For example, when your health is failing, or your marriage is falling apart, "have faith" can feel like an empty phrase that doesn't yield what our hearts and souls need now—relief. To pinpoint why faith is so tough for Christians today, I could boil it down to two words: no evidence. Faith doesn't often show us what we need to see in the moment. Faith isn't tangible. And frankly, a lot demands our attention: politics, family issues, careers, hurt and pain, and the world's tribulations.

"Go," said Jesus, "your faith has healed you."
Immediately he received his sight and followed Jesus along the road.

—MARK 10:52

What does faith look like in a world of immediate gratification and pills that we can pop when we need to feel better?

What does Christ say about faith? What is faith exactly?

I've had many opportunities to come face-to-face with faith over the years and learn with God the power that faith can have in our lives. Years ago, our church faced a challenge that required what I would come to call Faith in Action. At the time, we were located in Robbinsdale, Minnesota, a smaller suburban community we'd grown to love, but felt we had outgrown. We wanted to reach more people, and had for years prayed that the right space would become available in the city of Minneapolis. When we finally discovered the perfect building, we knew we had a lot working against us. There was at least another group vying for the building we desired. A large corporation had previously owned the building, and a group that was interested in it were pretty close to securing the deal. On paper, they were likely a good candidate, especially because the purchase required quite a bit of money upfront. We believed that although we didn't have the two million dollars, we needed to buy this building—that it was ours—and that God would make a way.

On the surface, purchasing this building seemed impossible, especially because on top of coming up with the money, we also needed to pay off the loan for the building we were already in.

Looking back, I have to admit that I was concerned, and for good reason, knowing God had a plan for our church that included this building. I remember sitting at my desk when my wife pointed to an advertisement on my desk for a brand-new bank that was seeking customers. Our bank at the time, although helpful, required a lot of red tape guidelines that seemed almost improbable to meet. When I think back to that day in my office, I'm still amazed. In the end, that bank agreed not only to finance our new loan, but to provide everything we needed to make our purchase possible, including funds to renovate the building to make it more suitable for a church. To this day, we've been told our circumstance was unique.

Faith in God, regardless of your fear and doubt, can change your life. After moving into our new church home, I recognized that fear is part of what we face when we activate faith.

> *Naturally, you'll be scared as you confront life's challenges, but at the end of the day trusting God is the only way to truly "have faith."*

Knowing that we simply can't physically take faith out of the closet and put it on with the rest of our clothing means we must have a deep knowing in our spirit that it's there. We have to lean into our faith, place it in the driver's seat of our lives, and know that God has our back, no matter how we feel. Having faith means depending on God moment-to-moment. Person-

FAITH IN ACTION

ally, I think God enjoys this dependence on Him, and praises it. Look at the dependence of Peter as Jesus commands him to walk toward him on water.

"Lord, if it's you," Peter replied, "tell me to come to you on the water."

"Come," he said.

Then Peter got down out of the boat, walked on the water and came toward Jesus. But when he saw the wind, he was afraid and, beginning to sink, cried out, "Lord, save me!"

Immediately Jesus reached out his hand and caught him. "You of little faith," he said, "why did you doubt?"

—MATTHEW 14:28-31

Think about it. In this moment, Peter needed faith to get out of the boat in the first place. And then, another layer of faith to walk toward Jesus without looking down, and then as he felt himself sinking, more faith to know that he would be saved.

> *The level of faith we're required to have is multi-dimensional, layered, and continual.*

More significant, Peter was the only man out of eleven who

stepped out of the boat.

I think one of the greatest drawbacks to faith are the opinions and actions of others.

- How often have you resisted being the first or only one to "step out of the boat" because those around you seemed quite comfortable where they were? I can only imagine what the disciples thought or might have said as Peter threw his leg over the edge of the boat to walk on water. "Man, you gotta be kidding me!" they must have roared from the safety of the boat.
- How many of us are surrounded by folks that don't see things the way we see them, or better yet, see what God is showing us? Our families, friends, and spouses mean well and give us their best advice from their perspective, but they're not God.

Every day, I believe there are moments where God holds His hands out to you, pleading for you to come to Him, trust Him, step out on faith, and believe in His promises for your life. He knows that you'll struggle with self-doubt, and think it too impossible to reach his hands as you walk over to Him, terrified of sinking into the waters beneath you. But He beckons anyway because He knows you can reach where He's taking you and see what He's showing you. You need only to know that as Jesus reached out and caught Peter, He'll catch you too.

As you read *Faith in Action*, I want you to give serious thought to how you define your faith. I want you to consider your faith actions day-to-day. When you wake up in the morning, what are your thoughts and behaviors? At work, with your children, and in your quiet moments with God, what does your faith look like? What are your conversations with God like? I wrote *Faith in Action* because I want us to see faith as what God

FAITH IN ACTION

intended—as an action word. Faith is a noun, but it is also a verb, asking us to "take action"—as in "believe, trust." You can apply faith in Christ and be transformed. Faith can do remarkable things—it can uproot your baggage and negative past, and activate your dreams. Faith can bring you closer to truth. It's time to apply real faith that works so that we can enjoy God and feel his presence as He enjoys us.

To say the words, "have faith" is not enough. Faith can be a powerful statement indeed, but your actions will move mountains, heal wounds, and crush your worries if you believe, trust, and depend on God. I'd be lying if I said Faith in Action is comfortable. Faith in Action will feel like a battle on some days, and like a chore on others. But, the return on your Faith in Action is priceless.

> *When your first instinct is to know that God is in control, no matter what your circumstances are, you will have reached a place of completion and wholeness. Peace is not possible without having trust in God.*

RICHARD D. HOWELL, JR.

May the God of hope fill you with all joy and peace as you trust in him so that you may overflow with hope by the power of the Holy Spirit.

- ROMANS 15:13

As you turn these pages, I hope you know that your journey is one that God fully intends to walk with you. You aren't alone. Your family, community, and church need your Faith in Action. They not only depend on your reliance on God to carry you through—they also depend on your prayers for their Faith in Action to bring them through. Be encouraged. And when all else fails, know that God's hands are reaching toward you. All you need to do is put your faith into action. Believe it or not, the Lord is speaking to you—and when the Lord is speaking to you, be sure to listen so you can hear his voice.

Faith
fāTH/

verb

1. To show complete trust or confidence in God.
2. Believe, trust.

noun

1. Belief and trust in and loyalty to God.
2. Fidelity to one's promises.
3. Belief in traditional doctrines of a religion.
4. Something that's believed with strong conviction, like religious beliefs.

Chapter One

THE FAITH MYTHS

Now faith is confidence in what we hope for and assurance about what we do not see.

—HEBREWS 11:1

William, an eighty-five-year-old, dear member of our church family, was recently diagnosed with lung cancer. After he was hospitalized for an infection, I went to visit him. Alongside his family and friends, I held his trembling hand and prayed in earnest that he would be healed. Not too long after my prayer, the doctors told us that William's infection was indeed gone. Oh, how we celebrated Will's testimony! God had answered my prayer. I went to church the day after receiving the good news and declared on stage before our eager congregation, "Will is healed! Hallelujah!" We had a wonderful time celebrating.

When William died three weeks later, I was disappointed.

In my heart-to-heart with God, I mused, "Why?" How could God not heal Will after my big announcement? I'd had faith that he would beat his cancer, and believed with all of my being that God would answer my prayer. But, God had indeed answered my prayer and the prayers of William's wife, family, and friends. His reply was simple: It was William's time to leave this earth and join Him in heaven. In my more than thirty years as a pastor, facing that truth has never been easy for me. Trust me when I tell you that it was challenging to process God's answer about Will. Once again, I asked God and myself tough questions about faith. I loved William, as I'm sure you've loved a dear one that you've lost. And you should've seen Will before his passing. He was sitting up and enthusiastically talking about buying a house with his wife. When I think about it now, I was immersed in a *faith myth*. Looking back, I assumed that because God took away William's infection, I was really hoping that somehow his cancer could also be eradicated. In William's case, should I have pursued the desire I had for his healing—or should I have pursued having faith in God? Habakkuk 2:4 tells us how the just shall live—not by desire or assumptions, but by faith. There's nothing wrong with my faith—or with God. The myth was wrong.

Now faith is being sure of what we hope for and certain of what we do not see.

—HEBREWS 11:1

The problems with faith start because *many of us don't know what faith is*. Further, our (mis)understanding of faith confuses our understanding of God. Ask any Christian to define faith, and you'll hear a barrage of conflicting answers. The biblical verse that best defines faith can be found in Hebrews 11:1, and yet I believe there continues to be countless misperceptions about it, and many people who still simply don't understand what faith means at all. I often feel the actual definition of faith is like a volleyball that's tossed back and forth over a net of confusion.

Our biggest problem is that, as Christians, we've become entangled in a web of myths about faith, mostly contingent on a condition or desired outcome we want for our lives or someone else's. Though we tend to love God unconditionally, we struggle with having unconditional faith in Him. As a pastor, I get it. We all want happiness, joy, prosperity, and deliverance from difficulties, and there's nothing wrong with this. However, in the process of pursuing comforts and wants, we've subscribed to what I call the Faith Myths. These misconceptions about the nature and role of faith attempt to hold God hostage, and to obligate Him to our agenda, our temporal understanding of life events, and our ever-changing cultural ideas about spirituality. These myths attempt to entrench God in a wrestling match that's immersed in a philosophy and belief structure that isn't fair. And let's be honest, the reason is that our misconceptions about faith are often not biblically based, but instead experience-based. And here's the deal: experienced-based faith is deeply flawed because it poses a grave danger to genuine faith. It creates a limiting mindset where we try to force God to prove that our beliefs, wants, desires, ideas and hopes are right and beyond reproach, no matter how off target they may be.

FAITH IN ACTION

> *It is not a terrible thing to have hope, but when hope becomes a personal agenda against divine will, it will pose a crisis to understanding God.*

Let me put it this way: if our spiritual well-being depends on God solving every problem, healing every physical ailment, removing every barrier, and eradicating all suffering, while also opening all doors to our every wish, we are missing the point. Sadly, we're also trying to back God into a corner. Not to mention that our faith should be allowed to flourish outside that box of conditions we've attempted to anchor to God. It's become easy to confuse faith with so many things that it's not. In fact, we've created an Americanized gospel where faith has become nationalistic and materialistic. In this era of "naming and claiming" our blessings, our vision of a holistic relationship with Christ mirrors the American Dream more and more every day. And here's the hard truth we're learning the hard way: Christ did not have today's America in mind when he died for us on the cross. Indeed, if we investigate Christ carefully, the days leading up to and on the day of his death, show us with painstaking perfection *what true faith in action is.*

Even though Jesus was relentless in his commitment to God's will, I don't believe that he found it easy to have faith. We can examine Jesus and instantly learn a couple of things about faith. First, that faith is a powerful tool to know God intimately, and second, faith is challenging. Although Jesus very clearly knew who he was and surrendered to his purpose, the Bible says Jesus's sweat "was like drops of blood falling to the ground" as he prayed on the Mount of Olives mere days before his death (Luke 22:44). He didn't have an identity crisis. In fact, Jesus had a perfect relationship with God. Yet, he still prayed, "Father, if you are willing, take this cup from me; yet not my will, but yours be done. (Luke 22:42)" Though committed to God's will, that verse suggests that Jesus wasn't gleefully anticipating the hardships ahead. He wasn't excited about the pain he'd endure or the wickedness he'd come face-to-face with, yet he surrendered to it. Jesus could have delivered himself from the brutality, agony, and suffering of the crucifixion, but he didn't do that. Did he want to? Did every fiber of his being wish his circumstances were different? Maybe. Jesus was human after all. But, he shows us through his submission to God's will the importance of pursuing God in spite of wants, circumstances, and ultimately our fragile humanness. The lessons Jesus taught us through dying on the cross dispel all five of the major faith myths we're up against today.

Myth #1: Good Things Happen When We Have Enough Faith

In the book of Job, Satan claims that Job is only faithful to God because He has blessed him immensely. This debate between the Lord and the Adversary seems to beg the question:

> *Do we receive blessings because we have faith, or do we have faith because we are blessed?*

The answer, according to the Bible, is neither. We must be faithful—as we are in marriage—both in sickness and in health. The relationship between blessings and faith is not linear; it is infinitely complex and known only to Him.

Growing up, I was taught that good things happen if your faith is strong. If you pray hard and long enough, God will grant you beautiful things. We've all fallen into this trap. It's hard to believe that God's love requires absolutely nothing. That the right things in your life—a loving marriage, a successful career, children who are all healthy and happy—are not a measurement of how strong your faith is at all. God blessed you! Rejoice and be glad that your life is stable, pleasant, and filled with much for which to be grateful. However, don't confuse God's grace with getting a gold star for having enough faith or faith that is strong. Life is not a vending machine in which you insert faith, and in return, receive nice things. Job found this out firsthand.

This myth misleads us into believing that our blessings are all about us—and that we somehow control how blessed we can become (or not become) based on faith. The truth is that faith is about persistence and continuity. There's no such thing as having "enough" faith, or "strong" faith, or "weak" faith that can be measured by the rewards that God bestows on you. Don't fall into this trap. Good things happen, and bad things happen, and God loves you through it all. We can't earn goodness or riches or healing through faith. However, your faith ensures that through good times and periods of abundance that you're tapped into the Source—God. True faith doesn't gauge your closeness or good standing with God. And thank goodness God doesn't operate that way. If He did, we'd all be in trouble and a lot worse off. Instead, God loves us unconditionally, and blesses us regardless of where we are in our faith walk. His love is eternal and everlasting. Your blessings are not evidence of God's love or lack thereof, nor are they an adequate measure of whether you should increase or decrease your faith. Faith can't be quantified. Jesus was satisfied with whatever God wanted Him to do. He did it without a personal agenda. He accepted God's plan for him by sacrificing his desires—including his desire to live. We have to be satisfied with God's will as well.

By the same token, often those without faith do succeed. We do not need to look farther than a newspaper or magazine to see examples of those who we feel are less God-fearing and more corrupt than us seeming to thrive. Job noticed this as well, lamenting, "Why do the wicked prosper / growing old and powerful?" It is only when we unsubscribe from the myth *that the most faithful people are the most blessed* that we can begin to better understand God—and ourselves.

Myth #2: Hardships Happen Because We Don't Have Enough Faith

In my pastoral years, I have encountered more experiences where there are no answers, and where God is not saying anything. How do you handle those crises? Some people drop out of church, and then lose their respect for God. Many new converts in the early stages of their relationship with God become very disappointed and feel betrayed when faced with hardships. When bad things happen, like an illness, tragic death, or catastrophic failure, I've often heard and have said myself, "God, how could you let me down? I had all the faith in the world." Witnessing terrible things happen to godly people, or feeling as though fasting and praying aren't bearing the results someone wants, has led some pastors to abandon their pulpits.

We tend to blame God for the bad things that happen. In my ministry, I've seen this time and again. When I recently presided over the funeral of a five-year-old killed in a drive-by shooting, I felt my emotions get the best of me and challenge my faith. But, the truth of the matter is that both sadness and happiness are emotions and faith is a state of mind. Emotions come and go, depending on the events of your day, your attitude, environment, and mindset. By their very nature, feelings can't be judged by your faith. Feelings are too fleeting and immersed in day-to-day trivialities.

Most of us have it backward, and we're allowing our tough circumstances to test our faith. When life falls apart, we often believe that our faith is under scrutiny—that it's a judgment from God on our not doing enough, or for letting Him down. On the flip side, we often respond to hardship by assigning faith the responsibility of making it all go away. In tough times, we frequently believe that our faith has something to prove to us. In reality, we don't have the power to test faith. Faith tests us. But naturally, when life kicks our butt, we call on God to show us deliverance from hardships and also that we are in fact loved, cherished, anointed—the list goes on. But we've got it wrong here. When we face difficulties, we need to do the reverse. Like Jesus on the cross, faith in action means we need to show God that whether we receive deliverance from our hardships or not, He is loved, cherished, and anointed. It's always about God, even in hard times. His presence is what I must constantly seek.

I know it's tough to think about faith in these terms, especially when you're knee-deep in an emotional, physical, or financial crisis. But what I've learned is that through all circumstances, including the bad ones, no matter what the breakthrough is that I desire or wish for, the answer is always to fear God. God is the key. God is the answer. God is also my focus, and His presence is what I must yearn for. It's not always easy.

But we must have faith despite the bad things that happen. We have to remain faithful when we don't understand why or how God could allow troubling events to occur. Sometimes I ask God why, but in tragic circumstances I've witnessed God in action. It's hard to explain God in those hard moments. Sometimes tragedies are resolved, the miracle that I prayed for happens, and things work out in a way that I had hoped and prayed for. But sometimes it doesn't. Regardless, we still have to pursue God's presence in our life, and to do so without believing that God is out to get us, or worse, responsible for our hardships. There has to be a reverence for God and trust in Him regardless of what we're going through.

If you look at almost every person in the Bible, they had to go through wrestling matches with God—Jacob, Isaac, Ruth, and Abraham to name a few—and yet they demonstrated true faith. They never gave up on God.

> *Don't think that your challenges occur because your faith is weak. That's simply not true. Faith in action means keeping your eyes on God and feeling His presence, especially when things aren't going well in your life.*

Myth #3: Faith is a Parachute

Another misconception about faith is that regardless of the choices you make, good or bad, faith will save you. We often talk about a "leap of faith"—in which we take a chance on something risky, and then bank on God to protect us from any negative consequences. We do this and claim that we are

FAITH IN ACTION

"trusting in God," but sometimes it feels more like a demand of God.

You can see how this thinking could be dangerous. This myth says you can marry a person that you know deep down isn't God's choice, but he or she will somehow become the perfect mate because of your faith. This myth is why you might have purchased a home you can't afford, believing that you'll magically be able to make the mortgage payments...if you have faith. Real talk: faith will not excuse our bad decisions. I know it sometimes feels better to believe that an unwise decision can be undone (or miraculously work out) if you have faith that it will. But wishful thinking (more about this in Myth #5) can't save you from something that isn't God's will for you. Sometimes poor choices work in our favor, and I truly believe that God can use anything for good—including divorce, abuse, addiction, and incarceration. The Bible is full of stories of hardship that all directly lead to the birth of our Savior. But we often make the mistake of leaping headfirst into a terrible situation, with the expectation that faith will bail us out in the end. Folks, the truth is that faith sustains us as we learn the lessons our mistakes teach us. It's the sustenance that keeps us connected to God when our choices fail us. However, faith doesn't protect you from yourself. Remember Jacob? Faith didn't prevent or excuse the sin of stealing Esau's blessing. Nor did faith miraculously transform theft into a good idea.

> *Thank goodness faith in action helps us pick up the pieces and know that God is in control no matter what mistakes we make.*

Myth #4: Faith Is a Magic Word

How often have we heard that by having faith, and merely praying for a blessing, that God will bring it to pass? The problem: essentially this means that some of us are more deserving or worthy of blessings than others. If I prayed for and received a promotion at work, and you also prayed for a promotion but didn't receive one, does that mean I'm more worthy in God's eyes than you are? Did I have "faith" the right way? And did you have "faith" the wrong way? Of course not. Faith is not a magic word that brings instant gratification. By faith, it's not likely that God will do everything you ask Him to do because He is not a fast-food restaurant, and faith is not a drive-thru intercom for you to bark orders through. Sure, God will answer your prayer, but His answer will be on His terms and in His timing. And frequently, the answer to your prayer is "No." God's answer will not always be what you want to hear, regardless of how strong your desire is. In other words, faith is not a guaranteed "Yes," from God simply because you want something really bad, even if you want something utterly, painfully justifiable, for example: a report of good health from the doctor, a restored relationship, or more years with your precious loved ones. Faith isn't a good luck charm that promises you anything at all. God opens doors. He at times opens doors that *you want to be opened,* but not always.

> Faith in action means trusting that God will open the right doors, close the wrong doors and that His timing is always perfect.

And remember: not every closed door is a bad thing. When Naomi lost her husband and her sons, it seemed that her life and her legacy were severed. But it was only through this tribulation that her daughter-in-law, Ruth, would go on to remarry and become the grandmother of David, whose bloodline continues down to Jesus Himself. Although a door closed for Naomi, a door opened for the salvation of all humanity.

Myth #5: Faith and Wish Are the Same Things

The mistakes we make when we confuse faith with a wish is probably the most dangerous of all the faith myths. A wish is an intense yearning or desire we usually want in the short-term. But here's the deal: faith is not temporal and tethered to our immediate earthly desires. When we look at faith, we have to think eternally. I'm not saying that we should abandon hope or that our wants are frivolous and meaningless to God. Hope is what we need to have in the short-term. But we place a lot of pressure and burden on our faith. The beauty of faith is that when your hope is gone or running low, and when a wish doesn't come true, faith guarantees your endurance, regardless of whether you're happy or not, or in a season of abundance or not. When you confuse wishes with faith, you lose yourself in the fury of your unfulfilled wishes becoming disappointments. Those disappointments become examples of how your faith failed. Your failed faith becomes a wedge between you and God, and makes you feel like quitting. Why bother having faith if God isn't listening, right? This cycle was never God's intention for faith. In fact, God intends for faith to be our most effective weapon in order to defeat disappointments.

Faith in Action:

- Knows that God will prevail no matter what. Wishes *don't stand a chance* against God's perfect plan for our lives.
- Is not losing your mind because you've lost something. Wishes become seeds of regret when we don't get our way. Regardless of what happens in your life, faith is what reminds you that you still have eternal life.
- Helps you trust in what you can't see.
- Is the voice that tells you, "God's got it under control. I'm not going to worry myself sick over this issue. It's in God's hands."
- Is the voice that that tells you that you may die, but you still can live; that you may be penniless, but you're still rich; and that you may have lost friends, but you still have the best friend you can have. The "but" in each of those statements is the faith part.

Your losses can still be your victories when you're pursuing God, regardless of what you see in front of you. When we subscribe to the faith myths, it's easy to give up. What you see in front of you makes you feel like God isn't in control—and that He's let you down. Do you see how the main difference between a wish and faith is that a wish stems from your will, and faith is steeped in God's will? You might wish that you had a new job or that your spouse becomes a Christian. But faith in action is surrendering to whatever the will of God is.

> *The mystery of faith **is not knowing** the will of God, and trusting Him anyway.*

FAITH IN ACTION

The pursuit of God is what guides you on this journey. Faith in action is the never-ending and persistent pursuit of God.

FAITH IN ACTION STEPS:

1. Accept.
Faith in Action is accepting God's answers to prayer across time and place.

2. Glorify.
Faith in Action is not based on the quantity of faith one has; instead, it's about praising God no matter what our circumstances are. See Philippians 4:13: *I can do everything through Christ, who gives me strength.*

3. Seek.
Faith in Action is seeking what God wants for us, not what we want from God. God gives us what we want, although it's not what we think we are seeking.

4. Believe.
Faith in Action believes that all good things come from God, on both good and bad days.

Chapter Two

FAITH: GOD'S PERFECT PLAN IN A MESSED UP WORLD

Why do you make me look at injustice? Why do you tolerate wrongdoing?

Destruction and violence are before me; there is strife, and conflict abounds.

—HABAKKUK 1:3

So, if faith is not a parachute, gold star, magic word, or a drive-thru window, then what is faith? Faith is trust in God. Period. It's not your agenda. It's not your philosophy. Faith is not about what you want to happen. Faith is putting your complete trust in God, no matter what. And trusting God means putting His wants before your wants. It's also trusting God's plan and wisdom in spite of things not turning out how you expected. If when you have questions (but you don't have answers), *faith is knowing that God knows best.* Faith is also trusting that all outcomes are in alignment with God's will, including when we don't like the outcomes, and don't understand them.If everything came up roses for everyone, faith would be so light and comfortable that it floated away. If bad things never happened, Earth would be Heaven. So faith doesn't come in spite of adversity; faith comes because of adversity. Faith, like a blade, must be sharpened against something tough and blunt and heavy.

> *God's plan is faith in Him and deferring to His power, which is the only true power. Faith brings light and humility. You want real peace? Trust God. You want real light? Trust God. Trust is what God wanted from the very beginning.*

But today, the state of faith is in complete crisis, especially in America. The higher an American's income, the greater the chance is that they don't believe in God. It seems silly when you think about it. Shouldn't the people who are the most blessed, and who don't need to worry about not having enough money to live, have the most faith? Shouldn't those who are the most blessed, at least with material goods, trust God the most? My theory is that wealth blinds people to God because money makes life easier, removing adversity that is necessary for faith. Perhaps, this is what Jesus meant when he said it was easier for a camel to go through the eye of a needle than for a rich man to enter the kingdom of God (Matthew 19:24). But if you look at the scripture more carefully, maybe it's not wealth that keeps the "rich man" from entering the kingdom, but rather a lack of struggle. When conflict is missing from our lives, we

FAITH IN ACTION

often close our eyes to the glory of God. And if our eyes are not opened wide, we cannot bask in His glory, which is as big as a camel is, when compared to the eye of a needle.

One of the most common attempts to disprove the existence of God is by citing the world's tragedies—slavery, the Holocaust, world wars. How could a compassionate God allow death, destruction, and evil to prevail? When we point to global tragedies, we can't fathom how they could fit into God's plan. And when we don't understand God's plan, we often use that as a reason not to have faith. But again, faith does not occur in spite of not understanding God's plan. Faith happens because of it. This assault on faith comes from the idea that our human logic is the source of truth. If Man cannot comprehend God's plan, he often disregards it completely. However, the fact is that if we understood God's plan—exactly how each trial in our lives was essential for executing His vision—then we wouldn't need faith.

But we do need faith.

The prophet Habakkuk was surrounded by injustice, evil, and sin. He was frustrated and in despair as he watched bad things happen to good people, and saw bad people rise. Habakkuk wanted to know why, and he questioned God, not once, but twice. His first question was essentially "God, how could you let this happen?" and the second question was "Why are the evil able to prosper?" Like Job, Habakkuk wanted answers. God explained that He had a plan, which included using the Babylonians—a corrupt and wicked nation—to bring about His will.

Understandably, Habakkuk struggled with this. He didn't like God's answer. We can all relate to this, right? Habakkuk went so far as to describe all the bad stuff around him. Habakkuk might have thought maybe God wasn't listening close enough. Surely, He could do something. Maybe He really didn't know how bad things were. But, God responded a second time to Habakkuk with the same response. Eventually, Habakkuk stopped asking. You ever notice how the more you question God, the fewer answers you seem to get? I think it's simply because we often don't want to hear God's answers.

Babylon, like many prosperous nations today, was consumed with its greatness. In fact, Babylon is compared to a drunkard whose appetite was never satisfied. By the third and last chapter of Habakkuk, we get a powerful illustration of faith in action. Habakkuk finally, surrenders. "The Sovereign Lord is my strength! He makes me as surefooted as a deer, able to tread upon the heights," (Habakkuk 3:12). He decided that since he couldn't control God, he might as well praise God, and instead have trust.

We are a curious people. We think we need to have all the answers. And curiosity isn't a bad thing, but we need to accept that there are answers we can never know. When you feel yourself questioning God's plan, refer to Job 38. Ask yourself, as the Lord asked Job: Have you comprehended the vast expanses of the earth? Do you know the laws of the heavens? Have you ever given orders to the morning, or shown the dawn its place, that it might take the earth by the edges and shake the wicked out of it?

Didn't think so.

Reason cannot be the thing we prize the most. That must be faith. Does it make sense that water can turn into wine, or that a man can walk on water? Of course not. That's what makes them miracles. Electrons can be in two places at once. If you could fold a piece of paper in half forty-two times, it would be thick enough to reach the moon. Shaq has only hit one three-pointer in his entire NBA career. The universe doesn't make sense. Why should we ever discount something because it doesn't make sense to us? Scientists still can't figure out why humans yawn.

If Man can't look upon the face of God without being overwhelmed by the glory—without dying—why would we think that the totality of His plan would be discernible to us (Exodus 33:20)? When, in Corinthians, the apostle asks, "Who has known the mind of the Lord...?" he's being rhetorical.

Look at what's happening in the political landscape today. We've got terrorism. We've got strife in North Korea. We've got political discourse right here in our country. This world often seems upside down. Is God allowing this to happen? Is God purposefully, intentionally, allowing this political riff-raff to happen?

I say, yes God is. He could stop it, but He won't. God allows tragic events to build our faith. Let's talk about Hitler. Did God allow the Holocaust to happen? Did God allow Hitler to annihilate millions of Jews? What about the killing fields in Cambodia where more than a million people were massacred? Did God let that happen? We may never know the answers to these tough questions. But, one thing is for sure. Tragic events like the Holocaust and wars often spark a revival. For example, after the Holocaust, Jews around the world became more united. Cambodia is also more unified because of a terrible and unimaginable crisis.

We don't like to talk this way. Like Habakkuk, we don't like to feel as though evil that we have no control over prevails. After all, that's not how it works in the movies; evil is supposed to be vanquished, the innocent saved, and the future secured. But if we're going to practice faith in action, we have to accept that God's plan is often beyond our understanding. That doesn't mean we should stay home during protests, or reject medicine, or avoid planning for the future. And it doesn't mean that we should feel like failures when, despite our best efforts, tragedy comes to pass. We should instead take comfort in the fact that God is in control, and while He may appreciate our righteous actions, He sees much further than us and knows best.

And here's another hard truth. Sometimes it takes a crisis to wake us up and call us back to God. When we don't like what we see happening around us, remember that faith in action recognizes that there's a reason for it, and it's often to fulfill God's ultimate purpose. Faith in action knows that no matter what, good always prevails.

Here's another way of putting it: we need to get rid of our agendas. We regularly refuse to accept what God has given us, and we pursue our earthly plans, always trying to climb higher and higher until we are in Heaven. But you cannot climb to reach God; you have to kneel to reach Him. And our earthly agendas seem always to be about gaining power, through wealth, or influence, or fame.

Almost every issue that plagues our world today comes from lusting for power. Discrimination and hatred often occur when a majority population wants to exert power over a minority population. Men assault women, physically and sexually, because they want to exert power. Police shoot unarmed people when they feel their authority over them is threatened. To boss people around because you have money, influence, or a badge is to play God. Often power can corrupt organized religion.

The crises that people have caused across the planet should make us more reverential of God. Only God could be entrusted with a surplus of power, and have the ability to use it so benevolently. The question is: how do we as flawed humans fight against the lust for power?

We must do the opposite: submit. And we must submit entirely. I'm not talking about submission to an earthly power—a politician, a police officer, an employer—for worldly power is not of God. Earthly power works in its self-interest, and not that of God. This doesn't mean we must always disobey—we should almost always follow instructions from police—but there is room for civil disobedience. The only being that we should submit entirely to is God.

Think back to 1 Samuel 24. While Saul hunts David, he unknowingly stumbles into a cave where David lies in wait. Although David could have killed Saul, he chose not to, because Saul was, in David's words, "the Lord's chosen one."

In this story, we see a righteous man put God's agenda over his own. Although he could have asserted a violent power over Saul and taken the kingdom for himself, he instead yields to God's plan. David could easily have defaulted to his strength, because after all, Saul was right there. But instead David did the right thing, and he demonstrates faith in action. He trusted that God would handle Saul His way and in His timing.

Often when we don't see God working on our timetable or in the way we'd want Him to control something, we try to take matters into our own hands. But, faith in action assures that God's presence is real, whether we see it or not. It means we can't become dismayed by the discouraging things we see. Hope, strength, endurance, perseverance against the struggle, adversity, questions, and stress, is what builds your character. You must have adversity to make your faith stronger. When we were created, it wasn't so that everything would happen our way. Faith in action is a journey to know God. Our purpose in life is to walk with God, and know that He is in control of our lives. We also need to enjoy God. Remember, God is not a mean God who hopes we slip and fall—He enjoys us. He wants us to enjoy Him all the time, but we often lose sight of this as we get impatient and focused on ourselves. But experiencing God is to bask in his pleasure—factoring him into our thoughts, dreams, peace, destiny. Real talk: We've got to get over ourselves and see God for who God is.

Nothing is easy. With the recent political chaos, I recently caught a TV interview of U.S. Senator Cory Booker. When asked by his interviewer, Joe Madison, whether he was frustrated by the current climate in the Senate, his response was spot on. He answered, "I expect conflict! That's a part of life, and that's where you draw your strength from." Booker couldn't have said it better.

> *Faith in action is expecting things*
> **not to go your way.**

What if we started thanking God for our problems? Instead of becoming frustrated that God isn't fixing things around us we think are broken, what if we instead saw troubles as an opportunity to depend on, and draw ourselves closer to Him? Faith is the most brilliant plan of God. In a world that often feels messed up, faith is our divine weapon. Although we can't always see, feel, or hear what we want from God, faith is our only way to overcome ourselves and truly have oneness with Him.

FAITH IN ACTION

FAITH IN ACTION STEPS:

1. Repent.
It is impossible to live in this world and remain blameless. There may have been times you have envied God's power and wanted the world to bend to your will. In your darkest times, you may have even wished someone harm. Faith in action is repenting for all the times you have wished for the power to make others submit to your will.

2. Denounce Distractions.
It isn't enough to simply atone for the things you have done and thought; you must consciously plan to do better, and then follow through on this plan. What are the distractions to your faith? What do you lust after? What circumstances cause you to question God's handling of things?

3. Declare Your Faith On Your Knees.
There are many ways to pray, but there's no better way to express your faith than to kneel; it is how we show that we are submitting to God. Bow your head. Do not look to the sky, because you cannot look upon the face of God.

4. Enjoy God Again.
Sometimes we think that pleasure can only come from having power, but there is also pleasure in submitting to God. There is joy in service. But, believe it or not, there can also be joy in thanking God for your problems. Start enjoying God on purpose, recognizing that your dependence on Him can provide countless opportunities to know and enjoy Him on a deeper level.

RICHARD D. HOWELL, JR.

Chapter Three

THE FAITH OF JESUS

Then Jesus said to him, "Get up! Pick up your mat and walk."

At once the man was cured; he picked up his mat and walked.

The day on which this took place was a Sabbath,

and so the Jewish leaders said to the man who had been healed,

"It is the Sabbath; the law forbids you to carry your mat."

But he replied, "The man who made me well said to me, 'Pick up your mat and walk.'"

—JOHN 5:8-11

If you want to observe faith up close, Jesus Christ is our best example. Christ navigated around all the pitfalls of humanity and, through the many miracles he performed, showed us what faith is. He was created to shake things up. If you read the New Testament closely, you'll see that his life's mission was to redefine faith.

Jesus was born into a particularly interesting era—and his timing couldn't have been better. The culture of the Israelites was very law-driven and established a hierarchy in which people with an official religious position were unquestionable experts on faith. The Pharisees corrupted the law of Moses, and began to introduce oral traditions that became the major focus and the emphasis, rather than the Old Testament. Faith was no longer honoring God as much as it was honoring Man. And with that, the Roman imperialistic government forced Israel to take sides—Caesar or God. The Israelites were meticulous about following the law, but they had lost their way, and no longer had a stable relationship with God.

The spiritual climate was secondary to the political environment dominated by Roman influence. The Jews were in desperate need of a refresher course in faith. When Jesus was born in that manger, the Jews had no idea what was coming. They didn't know that Jesus was born to correct what had been done to God's law—to introduce a faith in God unparalleled to man, unparalleled to politics, unparalleled to society. The man, Christ, would demonstrate the kind of faith that was missing. The man, Christ, put his faith in action.

As Jesus became popular, the Pharisees quickly wanted Jesus to become "one of the boys." After all, at the height of his popularity, Jesus drew crowds in the thousands, and had quickly become known as a miracle worker. Who wouldn't want a man of that magnitude on their team? The Pharisees figured that in Jesus, they could gain a powerful voice for their cause, and that he would provide them recognition. The Bible says that when

Jesus taught, he taught with authority. There was something different about Jesus, and the Pharisees wanted to exploit it. When Jesus explained scripture, works, and life, he mystified and amazed both the Jews and Romans.

For starters, Jesus's faith was not socially, politically, or economically charged, which was standard for the day. Jesus's faith was theocratic specific. An example of this is how he forgave an adulteress when the law said to stone her (John 8:11). But we learn from the Scripture that faith is not about imprisonment or condemnation. Jesus didn't care about critics or public opinion. His faith drove him to forgive a woman who'd committed adultery. We see this again in Luke 7:36-50. We're told that a "sinful" woman washes Jesus's feet with her tears. The Bible doesn't say, but we believe that she was a woman of the streets. Therefore it would have been a big deal for this particular woman to have been allowed to do this. It's an even bigger deal that Jesus forgives her, saying, "Because you believed, you are saved from your sins. Go in peace." This was not a political exercise. This is faith in action demonstrating that because Jesus knew God's plan for him and for all us, he was obligated to show love, kindness, and mercy. Again and again we witness Jesus practicing what I call the *Faith in Action Formula: being mentally tough, emotionally strong, and physically fit as he handles each God-appointed assignment.*

Jesus taught us that faith doesn't run away like a jackrabbit. When I learned that my dad, who was fighting cancer, might be able to take radiation, I was happy. On the day of his first treatment, I went to the clinic to be with him. When I walked in, I thought it was odd that there were no cords or machines. I noticed my dad having a conversation with his doctor and my mother. I'll never forget the look on the doctor's face as he told

FAITH IN ACTION

us there was nothing more to be done. The cancer had spread. They decided radiation wasn't a good option for my dad, after all, fearing it would make matters worse and could kill him. My father, sitting there in his wheelchair started crying, quietly muttering, "Jesus." He didn't complain, or ask God why. The mental toughness my dad demonstrated at that moment showed his faith in God, and that he was not going to allow liver cancer to shrink his faith. He gave God glory in the toughest moment of his life.

Therefore, since we have been justified through faith,

we have peace with God through our Lord Jesus Christ.

—ROMANS 5:1

> *Faith is accepting the entire reality,*
> *but knowing it is driven by God's plan.*

That's what Jesus demonstrated, and I saw it up close with my dad. Of course, Jesus's greatest test of faith was submission to death. He was delivered to this world to die. Why? Because it was God's plan. The scriptures foretold it. At any time throughout his assignment, Jesus could have run away. Think about it. At any time he could have said, "Never mind, I'm not going to do this." The man had proved himself capable of doing the impossible; even when he was up on the cross, he probably could have done away with the nails piercing his hands and feet, and climbed down. But he didn't. There was never a time when he considered doing so. He wrapped his faith in God. It was non-contingent, non-negotiable, and he was strictly obedient and submissive to God. He hurt, suffered, and bled, but he never ran away, demonstrating faith in action.

We can't talk about the faith of Jesus without addressing his mental toughness. Today, many of us question our Christian identity and our destiny. We examine the burden of our God-given assignments, and struggle endlessly to discern its meaning. When God asks us to do something, the mental battle is often harder than the spiritual. Think of Jonah, who in response to God's request, essentially said, "I know what you told me God, but I'm not going to do it. I don't want to be embarrassed." We know Jonah eventually came around, but not without God's intervention. But Jonah isn't unique. We've all been there. Following the will of God is tough. But when we follow our minds instead of God, we fail Him. After all, submission is hard. But that's the mental stuff Jesus wants us to overcome.

> *Faith in action is deciding against all the odds, pain, suffering, bad news, and messiness that God's plan **is your plan.***

But the deal is that His plan requires mental toughness. Your thoughts are going to come against you in tough times. You'll be tempted to give up, throw in the towel, and take the path of least resistance. But challenge your mind to stay focused. And

FAITH IN ACTION

in moments of despair, think of a starving and tired Jesus being tempted in the wilderness by Satan. Jesus said to him, "Away from me, Satan! For it is written: 'Worship the Lord your God, and serve him only.' Then the devil left him, and angels came and attended him" (Matthew 4:10–11). In the moments where mental toughness seems beyond your reach, as Jesus did, tell your negative, self-pitying demons "Away from me!"

But what about our feelings? We all get angry, depressed, sad, worried, and fearful. It's difficult to activate our faith when we're not emotionally strong. Our feelings play a big part in our day-to-day journey as Christians. Can you imagine the emotional strength of Jesus as he was dragged through the streets with a cross on his back, and then nailed to it? Can you imagine the thoughts running through his mind and the feelings coursing through his body as he passed through crowds of taunting people? Jesus was the epitome of faith in action at that moment. He'd accepted his fate, and wasn't a minute late for his assignment. He didn't reconsider or wonder about what would befall him. Jesus always knew the precise moment he would be apprehended. What would you do if you were him? Jesus was right where he was supposed to be, watching his disciples up to the moment before he was arrested. He also advised Judas to go through with betraying him. That's deep, right?

In Jesus's final moments, we learn quite a bit about his emotional resolve. When you think about it, Jesus's feelings could easily have betrayed him. But what he shows us is that our feelings are often a cop-out. Though we often know what we need to do, we still choose not to. We might say, "I'm supposed to study, but I don't feel like studying today," "I'm supposed to be at work, but I don't feel like working today," or "I'm supposed to be a good husband, but I don't feel like doing that today." We use our feelings as our escape clause.

> *Faith is mental, but it's also emotional.*

I have been crucified with Christ and I no longer live, but Christ lives in me.

The life I now live in the body, I live by faith in the Son of God,

who loved me and gave himself for me.

—GALATIANS 2:20

Here's where passion comes in. When our emotions are pulling us in a different direction than what God wants, we must remember our passion for God. That's what Jesus had. He was a passionate servant. The next time your feelings tell you to operate outside of God's plan, tap into your passion for Him. Remind yourself of God's everlasting love and presence. As my dad did, you might need to speak Jesus' name out loud so you feel his presence in the toughest of times.

Another example of faith in action is seen in Jesus's physical strength. In today's America, our physical well-being is in trouble. Though you might not see this as related to faith, I assure you it is. Look to Philippians 3:19: "Their destiny is destruction, their god is their stomach."

FAITH IN ACTION

When you see a fast-food restaurant on the side of the road, and you feel your stomach call out for you to stop at the drive-thru, you make your stomach your god, dictating your actions. We trust the cravings of our stomachs more than we are confident in God these days. How many of us listen to the voice of God within ourselves as often as we listen to our stomachs? The Bible condemns gluttony—so when we overeat, we are making a decision to worship the god of our stomachs over the real God.

Our bodies are going to pieces. We hunch in front of screens all day, and we don't exercise—when the Bible says, "The soul of the sluggard craves and gets nothing" (Proverbs 25:27). We drink too much, drug ourselves, and don't treat ourselves with respect and love. We're not in good health. Jesus was never addicted to nicotine or alcohol. His body was in alignment with his emotional strength and his mental toughness. It had to be in order to accomplish God's plan. Have you ever heard about Jesus being ill? I imagine if Jesus had the flu, he'd take care of himself. If you read the Gospels, you'll notice that Jesus ate right, and did a lot of walking, often for miles. He *even* walked on water.

We also learn about Jesus's faith in action through how he handled his ability to speak to groups without the public offending him. We're all driven by others' feelings and thoughts. We all want to be liked and respected. We don't want to be the loose cannon or the oddball in the group. We all want to be accepted. We want to belong, which is why we have sororities, fraternities, political parties, and boardrooms. However, like Christ, we cannot allow people to crowd our faith. Like him, we have to be our own person. Jesus was his own God, and we have to follow that example.

If you remember nothing else, remember that when you were born again, you signed up to follow God's plan. Everything that happens in your life has a reason and a purpose, and God's purpose is explained through experience. Faith in action develops the purpose of God, so do what you're supposed to do. Be obedient to your parents and your employer, serve your family faithfully, and take responsibility when it's given to you. These are all steps that lead to intimately understanding God's plan.

Lastly choose God, not society. In John 5, Jesus healed an invalid on the Sabbath. This was in violation of the "rules." Yet which is more important? Putting faith in God, or putting faith in public opinion? Jesus did not allow the opinions of others to distract him from doing in his heart what God had instructed him to do. All over America, we stop short of fulfilling our destinies because of others. Dreams have been shattered because of manmade barriers. Many people still have yet to dare to dream and step out of their comfort zones. Faith in action is stepping out of manmade obstacles to experience miracles. Disavow the naysayers and resisters. Get them out of your life…Now!

Whoever believes in the Son has eternal life, but whoever rejects the Son will not see life, for God's wrath remains on them.

—JOHN 3:36

FAITH IN ACTION STEPS:

1. Walk in Your Assignment.
Christ defied the odds of humanity to show us how to faithfully follow God's will. Follow Christ's ultimate example of submission to the cross. When God asks you to do something, don't run; rather, be obedient, and do not succumb to the mental and emotional battles that you might face.

2. Practice Mental Toughness.
Though it may be difficult, keep your mind trained on God when facing challenging times. Remember that God's presence never leaves you. When your mind is under attack, fight fire with fire. Do as Jesus did and tell negativity, "Away from me!"

3. Be Emotionally Strong.
Faith in action is overcoming your feelings. Emotional strength is built over time through constant communion with God. Pray for strength when you feel weak. Ask God to remove barriers. Whether feeling fearful, worried, anxious, or doubtful, have an arsenal of verses to refer to when you need them most. I refer to Joshua 1:9: Have I not commanded you? Be strong and courageous. Do not be afraid; do not be discouraged, for the Lord your God will be with you wherever you go. Also see 2 Chronicles 15:7, Psalm 27:1, and 1 Corinthians 16:13.

4. Get Physically Fit.
Faith requires fitness. Your mental and spiritual well-being depend on your physical health. Follow Christ's example, and treat your body as the temple of God. Refer to 1 Corinthians

6:19–20 where it says: Do you not know that your bodies are temples of the Holy Spirit, who is in you, whom you have received from God? You are not your own; you were bought at a price. Therefore, honor God with your bodies.

But the fruit of the Spirit is love, joy, peace, patience, kindness, goodness, and faithfulness.

—GALATIANS 5:22

Chapter Four

FAITH: THE POWER IN US

Jesus answered, "I am the way and the truth and the life. No one comes to the Father except through me."

—JOHN 14:6

There is no question that our world is changing. Across the planet, cultures are moving towards a secularized society, which leaves some Christians in doubt, and others in despair. Where does Christianity fit in today's culture?

The Bible is very straightforward. Jesus said, "Have faith in God"—and that faith does not adjust or fluctuate. No matter the season, political climate, or culture, faith in God never changes. We know that scriptures condemn alternatives to Christ. All roads lead to him. Jesus said, "I am the way, the truth, and the light." There is no other way to God but through Christ.

The last time I checked my Bible, one man had died on the cross and was buried, and the same man rose again. I never found anyone else in history that did what Christ did. No philosophy or invention or fashion has ever been as incredible as the story of Jesus of Nazareth. You can look through hundreds of pages of *Ripley's Believe It or Not* and never find an event as awe-inspiring. When Jesus said, "I am the way," it verifies his credibility without question. Christians need to examine their attitude about God. Is it holistic and pure, or is it mixed with other philosophies and other statements against God?

When Jesus said we needed to have faith in God, he meant it. Is there anything about those words we don't understand? He didn't say have faith in politics or schools of thought; he said it directly. I attest that Christians today must value what God has given them in order to believe. If we believe that God raised Jesus from the dead, which is the basis of our faith, we can also rest comfortably, assured that it's all right to have faith in him. Our attitude must rest in the gospel of Jesus Christ. We walk by Him, not by our sight.

But people are finding new centerpieces for their lives, filling in the space where God should be. Some people believe their world revolves around money. Others worship themselves. One centerpiece I see most often *is pain*. Think of Naomi, who renamed herself Mara, which means "bitter." She redefined her identity around that bitterness, her pain, her hurt. She never wanted anyone to address her again with her given name—which means "pleasant"—because she consciously chose bitterness over pleasantness. She didn't realize that the Lord had not given up on her. She did not realize that she was to be a direct ancestor of Christ. She did not realize that *her pain* would be a tool for God to execute his divine plan.

I'll be very frank with you; some people can't live without being hurt. They enjoy the attention that is drawn to their hurt and their pain—because that's all they know. Another case is in John, which used the example of the invalid who had been ill for his entire life, and it was all he knew. But a cure was available at a pool not far from where he lived. According to the scripture, "An angel went down at a certain season into the pool, and troubled the water: whosoever then first after the troubling of the water stepped in was made whole of whatsoever disease he had." Again and again the man tried to get to the healing waters, but every time, someone would get in before him. You need to give the man credit—*at least he tried every year.*

But Jesus came across this man and asked him, "Do you want to be made whole?" but the man didn't say "Yes." He did not affirm that he wanted to be healed, instead saying, "I can't." He was so conditioned to his hurt and pain that he couldn't see that Jesus was ready to heal his body.

People live in pain because that's all they know, and pain does have a ministry. Pain can be habitual. Even when a person is not in pain, she lives in pain. She works off of pain, she socializes in pain, and she works through pain. But all her pain is and ever was, is an experience.

The very impact of pain without faith places serious concerns which leads to disastrous consequences. Judas Iscariot's pain in feeling overlooked led him to betray his very Lord. We all need to re-up on our faith and help those around us do the same—because people need faith.

RICHARD D. HOWELL, JR.

Dear friends, do not believe every spirit, but test the spirits to see whether they are from God, because many false prophets have gone out into the world.

—1 JOHN 4:1

Here's an example: Alcoholics Anonymous (AA) has helped millions of people quit drinking, using their twelve-step program. Over half of these steps indirectly reference God and our need to recognize His power over us, some of which, like step three (Make a decision to turn your will and your life over to the care of God), should sound a lot like what we've been talking about. Often people who do not have a relationship with God will join the program because of how successful it has been at helping alcoholics manage their illness. Researchers have found that the program works, regardless of whether the participants are people of faith or not—until tragedy strikes.

We've talked a lot about hardship and adversity in the previous chapters, and this is a concrete example of why we need God in tough times. Often AA doesn't work if you don't have faith.

Researchers at UC Berkeley, Brown University, and the National Institutes of Health found that:

> *"Alcoholics . . . could often stay sober until there was a stressful event in their lives—at which point, a certain number started drinking again, no matter how many*

new routines they had embraced. However, those alcoholics who believed . . . that some higher power had entered their lives were more likely to make it through the stressful periods with their sobriety intact."

This should come as no surprise to us.

> When you trust God, even through tough times, you can cope with a tragedy that would send nonbelievers into a downward spiral.

Faith can heal people. Faith can help people heal themselves. And this is good news worth sharing.

Harold Koenig, the author of *The Handbook on Religion and Health*, documented over a thousand studies done on the effects of prayer on health, and concluded that people who pray get sick less often. They also recover more quickly from depression, and also have shorter hospital stays.

Faith is good for people. Hopefully, you know this from your own experiences. Hopefully, you've felt—more than just the quantifiable scientific benefits—the warmth and security of God's embrace. We cannot lose our faith right now, and we cannot let those around us lose their faith either. Mass shootings are on a rise. Both major political parties are fractured. Tensions with the police are as high as they've ever been. Now that things look most dire for our country, we need to trust in God to see us through the turmoil.

I know it isn't easy, but I like what was said in Jude 1:3: "I felt compelled to write and urge you to contend for the faith that was once for all entrusted to God's holy people." The Greek word for "contend" is "epagónizomai," which means "struggle." Struggle for the faith. Fight for the faith. It is not enough to have faith; we must put our faith into action.

When thorns of doubt invade your mind, do not simply let them strangle your faith. Struggle against the doubt. When a friend has lost his way, fight to set him back on the path to the Lord. Help him struggle for his faith. There will always be pain in that fight, but you have to know that there is truth in that pain. Your pain is not God, but God is in your pain. There is truth in your weariness. You can crush it to pieces, but it will still abound as truth. That's what Jesus walked with, what the apostles, the fathers of our faith walk with, and you have been called today to walk in that same faith. Seeking comes through challenge. The many problems that come against your faith are training you to gain more faith. You find faith through your crises and your challenges.

We have power in us that will help us in this struggle. This power is in all of us, believe it or not, but most of us just don't know we have it. We're all walking around with a superhuman strength in us, lying dormant until we choose to acknowledge it. That power is Jesus Christ. It's the same force that we talked about earlier that helps people quit drinking or beat depression. This power wraps around us like a suit of armor; the greatest tragedies can hurt us, but cannot break us. You can see the power of God by looking at what you've been delivered from, prevailed over, and overcome. Simply seeing and reflecting on those things can give you insight into trusting God. This power is our most inalienable right. Look to Psalms 139:

FAITH IN ACTION

"Where can I go from your Spirit? Where can I flee from your presence?

If I go up to the heavens, you are there; if I make my bed in the depths, you are there." The power of God is with us even at our lowest point.

And we have a responsibility to use that power to trust God and to serve God fervently.

FAITH IN ACTION STEPS:

1. Evangelize.
Faith is good for people. Faith helps us deal with all the tragedies in our lives. If you love your neighbor like the scripture asks of you, and they are going through a tough time, help them find the power of God.

2. Assess Your Faith.
Think back—was there ever a time in which you had stronger faith in God than you do now? If so, find a way to recapture your belief. Our faith should grow throughout our lives, the longer we walk with God.

3. Thank God for Faith.
The greatest blessing is not losing trust in God. Thank God for your faith as Paul did. For inspiration, read Philemon 1:4-5: I always thank my God as I remember you in my prayers because I hear about your love for all his holy people and your faith in the Lord Jesus.

4. Reflect On Your Pain.
You've been through tragedy before. We all have. But hopefully, you've managed to keep God at the center of your life instead of redefining your life around pain. Ask yourself: Why did God give me the pain in my life? Dig deep, and see what goodness has come or may come in the future because of your pain. If you can't see the light at the end of your tunnel, that's okay. Believe there is light, and his name is Jesus Christ.

FAITH IN ACTION

Consequently, faith comes from hearing the message,

and the message is heard through the word about Christ.

- ROMANS 10:17

Chapter Five

THE GOD WARS

I will increase the number of people and animals living on you, and they will be fruitful and become numerous.

I will settle people on you as in the past and will make you prosper more than before.

Then you will know that I am the Lord.

—EZEKIEL 36:11

Ezekiel 36:11 holds special meaning for me. It helped me at a particular point in my life when I was caught in what I call a God War. I was struggling, asking God tough questions, and at the time, I felt that although God was hearing me, He wasn't providing answers. Sound familiar? I was in crisis. My entire life was affected, and my understanding of God was shifting. I felt like I didn't know him as I thought I should, and you can imagine for a pastor this was a rough place to be. I had known God since childhood; however, as the years and months passed, I felt farther from Him than I ever had. My understanding of faith was undergoing a transformation. I remember believing earlier in my life that faith was *merely knowing God*. How wrong I was.

We've all heard the Sunday school stories and testimonies about how God always comes through and answers our prayers. I still believe that, but on a different level.

> *God doesn't always answer prayers the way you want Him to.*

You also don't always get the same answer for the same question. This goes back to those myths we discussed in chapter 1. There is no such thing as having "enough faith," and you certainly can't earn a better outcome based on the amount of faith you have. It's simply not the way God deals with us. What happens when you're in the middle of a God War?

When I found myself knee-deep in a spiritual crisis, I discovered when I began questioning God I opened up Pandora's Box. In fact, I exploded into question-binging. I asked myself: If I have this faith, then why am I spiraling in a cycle of doubt, distrust, and worry? Am I anointed? If so, I urged, then why am I going through this crazy stuff? God, are you still with me? Is this the end of my life?

> *Worry doesn't go with faith. Fear doesn't go with faith. Trust does.*

And yet, there I was worrying, doubting, contemplating, and questioning whether I had "real" faith in God. I'm no different than any other Christian. Like you, I also question God. Does questioning God mean that we lack faith? Or that we doubt God? To answer this question I looked more closely at the Bible and at what's called the imprecatory song.

Imprecatory singing is essentially complaining to God. To imprecate means "to invoke evil upon or curse" one's enemies. In fact, King David, the Psalmist, wrote imprecatory verses such as Psalm 55:15, 69:28, and 109:8. He used phrases like, "may their path be dark and slippery, with the angel of the Lord pursuing them" (Psalm 35:6) and "O God, break the teeth in their mouths; tear out the fangs of the young lions, O LORD!" (Psalm 58:6).

King David had no qualms about groaning and moaning to God. I happen to think this is okay. We can throw our problems and grievances in God's face. We can even rebuke our enemies to God. He can handle it. In the middle of my God War, I really mouthed off. There was no "Heavenly Father in the Name of the Lord Jesus Christ" to begin each prayer. None of that! I was in the midst of a face-to-face wrestling match with Him. I think that's what a crisis does. It brings the walls down. This is why our God Wars can often serve as a sign that God is demanding us to know Him more. A crisis can, in fact, produce a divine encounter.

This is what happened to me. In the middle of my God War, I learned that I didn't deny God my faith. When you're experiencing a God War, it's not that you don't believe He exists. There is no question of whether or not there is a God. For me, the question was: Why am I going through this? Why am I suffering? I thought I haven't done anything wrong. I'm trying for

God all the days of my life! Surely goodness and mercy should follow. Have you ever felt that way? You're reading the right scriptures, doing the church thing, and doing the faith thing. Then why is your current crisis so hard? You're trying not to say the wrong thing because, like me, you have been taught never to talk of defeat when you're in a God War. But you still feel like giving up. You're all out of answers. When you hit rock bottom, what do you do? Do you thank God or do you question Him? Well, I wondered, so I asked, "God what do you want me to do?" I was desperately searching for an answer. Finally, God responded, "Get your Bible and open it up."

His message came through loud and clear. But here's the deal, I've never liked doing that. Randomly opening the Bible to find the "right" verse always felt like reducing the Bible to a Magic 8 Ball. With more than thirty thousand scriptures in the Bible, what if I opened my Bible and the scripture I landed on had no relevance to the question I was asking or problem I needed to be solved? I could open the Bible and land on that one scripture that reads, "Judas hanged himself." I could open up to another scripture that says, "Go and do likewise." Besides, you don't always know if where you land is God's divine intervention. All these thoughts plagued me after I heard God's explicit instruction. I hesitated even though I knew it was God.

RICHARD D. HOWELL, JR.

> *And without faith it is impossible to please God, because anyone who comes to him must believe that he exists and that he rewards those who earnestly seek him.*
>
> **—HEBREWS 11:6**

Then I heard His voice again, and it said much more clearly, "Open your Bible." This time, I knew I wasn't mistaken, and I had better listen. As doubt crept in, I grabbed my Bible. I tried to be careful, being cautiously aware of not wanting to be guided by prejudice. I was nervous, and my fingers were shaking. "Oh gosh, I don't want to go through with this," I said to myself. Then I decided I'd trust God to lead me to the exact scripture he needed me to read. I was in a God War after all, and I needed His help. When I opened my Bible, my eyes immediately landed on Ezekiel 36:11.

After months of searching, this was the crowning moment of my prayer life. This time, He not only answered my prayer, but he also favored me with the precise scripture I needed at that moment. It meant so much to me. In fact, I wrote the date down in my Bible. It was like God entered the room and assured me Himself with a specially crafted message sculpted specifically for me in the depth of my own personal hell. Like Jonah, I was in the so-called belly of the whale. Right in the middle of an intense wrestling match with God, he led me to a scripture that spoke exactly to what I was questioning. The verse read:

FAITH IN ACTION

I will increase the number of people and animals living on you,

and they will be fruitful and become numerous.

I will settle people on you as in the past and will make you prosper more than before.

Then you will know that I am the Lord.

—EZEKIEL 36:11

My crisis had gone on for months. I felt like the Energizer Bunny . . . I was going and going and going, trying to fight my way to peace. No matter what I tried, I felt like I wasn't getting an answer. I'd tried keeping myself positive and hopeful, rebuking suicidal thoughts and depression, trying to be the man God called me to be. But, nothing helped me deal with this spiritual crisis that continued to nag at me. It was like a mosquito. I'd swat it away, but it wouldn't leave me alone. Every Sunday, I'd declare, "This is the day! This is the day for a miracle!" But nothing happened. The feelings were still there.

Ezekiel 36:11 was the miracle I had been seeking. When I opened up the Bible to that scripture, I knew God had heard me. Like in the book of Jonah, where he kept going down, and then down, and then down again, that's exactly how I'd felt. Jonah went down to Joppa, and then he went down into the belly of the ship until finally, he went down into the belly of a whale. What a serious cycle of downs! This special moment with God and my Bible showed me that leaning on God, especially when you're in a downward spiral, brings about a different level of faith.

Sometimes, merely hearing God's voice while you're in descent, is faith in action. When you're struggling to leave tenement housing, overcome a disease, have your children taken away, or lose your job, and you feel like nothing has changed, perhaps your faith is descending to a level of unbelief and disgust—this is when God wants you to strain to hear His voice. The act of seeking Him is a faith in action tactic that will transform your relationship with God.

I experienced this very transformation. It led to a new level of worship and thanking God. Being led to Ezekiel 36:11 at this crucial moment showed that first of all, God heard me; secondly, God spoke to me; and thirdly, even though the conditions didn't necessarily change overnight, He assured me. Now, you might ask why do we go through God Wars in the first place.

- In the case of Moses, he almost had a nervous breakdown in the wilderness. He was so overwhelmed, he asked God to take his life (Numbers 11:10-15), and then God answers him.
- Elijah, after a successful campaign at Mount Carmel against the prophets of Baal, defeated the prophets that sat at Jezebel's table. He was a victor, but the next day he was running scared, afraid for his life (1 Kings 19:3). He wants to die!
- Jeremiah also gives up at one point.

The list of prophets and biblical teachers in the Bible who fought God Wars is long. What is the logical answer for why God allows us to go through a crisis of faith? What is the purpose of a God War? Why must we come to the place of throwing hope to the wind?

FAITH IN ACTION

There can only be one answer. We go through God Wars to embellish our worship. They help us to learn to trust Him, regardless of circumstances. They show us that God is with us all the way. If you're in a victorious position where perhaps God has brought you to a Promised Land in your life, you still have no guarantee that you won't find yourself in moments of descent. In fact, I can guarantee that you will. Those are the moments when you need to turn up your worship. Ask yourself, "Is God worth giving up? Can I quit on my faith?"

For the record, when I talk about worship, I'm talking about adoring God, putting Him first, and recognizing that your life is about following His way and not your ways. If you remember, before David lost his first son with Bathsheba, he fasted in the hope that God would heal his son. David's son died anyway. David's actions after this are deep. He worships God (2 Samuel 12:20). As much as we hate descending, worship is how we ascend.

The God Wars creates a personal conflict. It's often a battle of what you believe to be true versus what you see in front of you. It's hard sometimes not to equate the two. You might also find that something is missing from what you learned in your earlier years as a Christian, and what's missing isn't helping you get through your current crisis. In our days as young Christians, we're often mesmerized by what we're taught. For example, I was taught that paying my tithes, faithfully attending church, and being obedient, would lead to a manifold of blessings. Now, I know that faith extends beyond being at the right place at the right time. God can meet you anywhere and anytime. Also, bad things can happen to us anytime. While it's biblical to pray, go to church, and seek God's face, it's not always faithful to think that God will deliver you from a crisis in your timing. Crises don't happen because we did anything wrong. In fact, I believe many of our crises happen because God loves us and the trying of our faith works in patience.

Here's the story of Gideon. He was a good man at a time when his people were apostates—religious backsliders. People who worshiped idols surrounded him. One day while Gideon was threshing wheat at harvest time behind closed doors in order to keep the Midianites from pillaging his harvest, God allowed the Midianites to steal his crop anyway. This led to poverty, degradation, and a community outcry, and ultimately hopelessness and despair. Gideon was victimized by the Midianites' bullish ways, which was why he threshed in private. After his ordeal, he understandably experienced a God War, and on a particular day, asked God the question of all questions: why? An angel appears and announces, "Gideon, thou mighty man of valor." Gideon was confused. He didn't feel like a man of great courage. He had been threshing wheat while hiding behind bushes. He probably thought, "Are you kidding me! God, I'm the exact opposite." He asks more questions and lists all the reasons he isn't this man of valor that God has proclaimed. He even reminds the angel of the reasons he's unworthy: he's the least in his family and from the tribe of Manasseh, which means overlooked. But, God had a task for Gideon anyhow—to deliver his people from the oppression of the Midianites. Gideon was overcome immediately. He wasn't ready and didn't think he was qualified for the task. His God War almost kept him from doing what God asked.

Gideon's God War is a bit different than feeling lost or oppressed by terrible circumstances. In Gideon's case, his God War was more about whether he was ready to rise to a God-given mission. Have you ever heard God's voice clearly tell you

FAITH IN ACTION

to move in a direction you didn't want to go? Have you ever wanted to stay put instead of uprooting your plans for the unknown? That was Gideon. His God War is completely relatable.

> We often feel like we're not ready, don't have enough time, or are simply unworthy of God's assignments.

In the end, Gideon needed two signs before finally doing what God asked. God assured him, with showing signs, and then Gideon followed God's instructions and was victorious.

What gives me comfort in this story is how God assured Gideon. God also assures us of His presence. If God doesn't stop your crisis, fix every problem to your liking, or make your life easy, He will still assure you. As doors in your life open and close, as you're asked to go in new and different directions, as you struggle through pitfalls and tribulations, as you wrestle with God, He will assure you.

FAITH IN ACTION STEPS:

1. Unleash Your Burdens.
When your days are dark, and you've hit a wall, remember that no matter how desolate your circumstances, God can meet you where you are. No problem is too difficult for God, and no grievance is too grave. As it says in Psalms 55:22: *"Cast your cares on the Lord and he will sustain you; he will never let the righteous be shaken."* Or in 1 Peter 5:7: *"Cast all your anxiety on him because he cares for you."*

2. Strain to Hear God's Voice.
In a God War, it's difficult to see the forest for the trees due to suffering and pain that can be debilitating. You might actually feel spiritual and emotional paralysis. But, these are the moments when your faith in action can simply be straining to hear God's voice. Perhaps, a Bible verse will be the way you hear His voice, or through a deep knowing in your spirit. Either way, focusing on the presence of God and His voice, will not only deliver peace, but keep you from sinking into an abyss of despair, confusion, and hopelessness.

3. Follow God's Instructions.
When God speaks to you, listen and then follow His instructions. Don't doubt, second-guess, or be swayed by your own desires. As you follow God, do not lean on your understanding as it states in Proverbs 3:5: *"Trust in the Lord with all your heart and lean not on your own understanding."* The act of following God, even as you might not understand the unknowns of what lies ahead, is the ultimate leap of faith.

FAITH IN ACTION

4. Be Assured.

In the depths of a God War, being assured of God's goodness and love can liberate you. In troubling times, the only thing you can know for sure is that God is God. As it says in Psalms 46:10: *"Be still, and know that I am God; I will be exalted among the nations, I will be exalted in the earth."* Though it may defy comprehension, remain confident that God is with you; remain assured that He is in control of your future, today, tomorrow, and always.

Chapter Six

THE TRANSFORMATIONAL POWER OF FAITH

And we all, who with unveiled faces contemplate the Lord's glory, are being transformed into his image with ever-increasing glory, which comes from the Lord, who is the Spirit.

—2 CORINTHIANS 3:18

I've said throughout this book that faith is a constant journey to God. Meaning, I believe God enjoys it when we pursue him. In fact, the Lord said in Matthew 11:28, *"Come to me, all you who are weary and burdened, and I will give you rest."* Ever since Jesus gave us direct access to God, we have had the most marvelous opportunity ever known to man—we can know God more. There's no complicated matrix or certain steps we have to follow to know Him. Although pursuing God may feel like a long and tiring race, remember it's a free race to God—and through the Holy Spirit, God has given us power from heaven to cross the finish line. The Holy Spirit is within us at all times and will never leave us or forsake us. He will be with us until the very end. When our journeys take us through tough terrain, we always have open access to God while we're on this earth.

As transformation comes through seeking God, we learn much more about this transformation looking at Romans 12:1: *"I beseech you, therefore, brethren by the mercies of God that you present your bodies as a holy sacrifice."* Holy is acceptable unto God. It is our right to present ourselves to God 24/7, unlike the old days when a person had to wait for a particular period to give animal sacrifices. In the New Testament, God says we can present our bodies to Him always. We have access to Him through the blood of Christ. But there's more. The next verse also tells us something truly profound. Read this carefully: *Do not conform to the pattern of this world, but be transformed by the renewing of your mind. Then you will be able to test and approve what God's will is—His good, pleasing and perfect will.*

Have you ever wondered what the transformation of faith through God truly means? If you were to give it deep thought as I have, you might come to a similar conclusion. Transforming means changing into a God-like you, with your intentions, motives, feelings, agenda, and communication reflecting God in all things. How close are we to that? Where are we in our faith walks? Are we at first base, second base, or have we not left home plate? Don't beat yourself up as you ponder this because when He came into our lives, God gave us faith to become more like Him day-to-day. I believe he intended this to be a journey. I haven't met a single person yet who perfectly reflects God. Faith in action is striving to be as much like God as I can, which I've learned to make a daily practice.

Saul in the New Testament was zealous, and he had a lot of pride and conviction. He believed all Christians were trouble, and he was present when the first martyred Christian was killed. He approved the stoning of Stephen, and then sought more Christians to arrest because he believed they were against the Law of Moses. He actually pulled them out of their homes to arrest and persecute them. With permission, Saul was on his way to Damascus to arrest more Christians. But, something happened when he heard a voice from heaven saying, "Saul, why are you persecuting me?" Notice carefully what the voice said. When Saul replied, "Who are you?" the voice responded, "I am Jesus, whom you are persecuting. Now get up and go into the city, and you will be told what you must do."

At that very moment of transformation, God had paved the way for Saul to be converted. However, the Glory of God blinded him, and he could not see, but God prepared the way for Saul's transformation. Then, God called Ananias, a good Christian man, but he had heard much about Saul's reputation, and hesitated to see Saul at God's command. But God assured Ananias it would be okay because Saul was a praying man. Ananias went to Saul and said, "The Lord has sent me to you. Receive your sight." In Acts 22 verse 15, we find out Saul was also baptized in the name of the Lord.

From there on, we don't find Saul picking up another brick or arresting another person. At that moment, his life began a transformation. He went from being the hunter, to the hunted. He realized that the things he once believed in didn't align with how God wanted to transform him. He saw his great need as becoming Christ-like. He pursued Christ as his model in understanding his transformation, knowing he couldn't conform to the world or its opinions because he saw the power in

FAITH IN ACTION

renewing his mind through Christ. He was challenged every day to have his life transformed, but that is what faith is. Nothing can transform a life but Christ. Nothing can transform a conscience but Christ. Nothing can transform personality and character but Christ. Saul admitted that there was nothing good in his flesh, and that evil was always present. He was constantly surrounded by temptations, opinions, obstacles, pressures, and stressors. But, nothing could hijack the power of God's transformation because his faith required submission.

Saul, who becomes Paul through his transformation, was a true disciple. He was an unapologetic follower of Christ. Once Christ's spirit is in us, there should be no desire to turn back. Instead, we should know that transforming into Christ is a process. Though we face daily pressures to throw our transformation to the wind, at the end of the day, a person connected to the Holy Spirit will always be determined through tears, questions, and downfalls to be like Christ. That is the real sign of faith—your dedication to Christ despite your circumstances. No exceptions, and no alternatives.

> *Faith in action is having an attitude of transformation.*

What on earth does an attitude of transformation look like? I believe God gives us a list of things to work on for ourselves. Sometimes, we don't want to acknowledge things we want to do in our lives. Maybe you think you talk too much or think too much. Whatever it is, the Holy Spirit continues to remind you of what to do. I'm still working on my attitude. For example, I tolerate backseat drivers, meaning I prefer not to be told how to drive or where to go, even when I'm driving in the wrong direction. Honestly, I'm still working on my patience for backseat drivers. However, I credit the Holy Spirit for showing me that I need to work on myself more. God allows countermeasures to come against us sometimes so we can see areas of our lives that need to be transformed. I've come to believe this: faith in action is submission to our list of things that we need to change.

Transformation is not always easy or pretty. It's like looking into a magnification mirror and seeing all the crevices, flaws, and enlarged pores close up that you usually don't see. You might not like the way your face looks when you see it magnified. And yet, up close, you see the real you. If you have yellow teeth or hair sticking up, you whiten them or slick your hair down. It's the same way when we face our mirrors of faith. God shows us these mirrors every day—the things we need to become better at, more aware of, and improve upon. Christ is in us, and we need to seek to be more like him. Faith in action will take us to many places in our lives. The common destinations include valleys and hills. Sometimes, we're going up the hill and sometimes we're going down. But don't consider your ups and downs as a strike against your faith. In fact, trials should be your measurement from God to show that He is with you.

> *Don't judge your successes and failures as enemies because they always teach you something.*

And whatever road you're on, remember that it is from God,

FAITH IN ACTION

whether in a valley, or on a hill, or the belly of a whale, remember this: Trust God. When you do, your faith will carry you through impossible odds that seem like the end of you, when in reality, it is an extension of you.

---

*For it is by grace you have been saved,
through faith - and this is not from yourselves,
it is the gift of God.*

—EPHESIANS 2:8

FAITH IN ACTION STEPS:

1. Be guided by the Holy Spirit.
Remember, you can do all things through Christ, and he will provide all the strength you need to become more like Him day-to-day.

2. Be content.
Learn to be content in every situation as you seek transformation. Know that facing your shortcomings is not easy, nor is it an overnight process. As you commit to becoming more like Christ, choose contentment over condemnation.

3. Trust your journey.
If you believe in Christ, you'll be transformed. Try not to compare your journey to someone else's, or assume that your journey will be like anyone else's. God created you uniquely and in His image. No matter your history or circumstances, God is with you on your journey to transformation.

4. Trust the Lord.
Remember all things work together for good. Christ is always working on us. When times are toughest is when you can be sure that God is working on your behalf. Becoming more like Christ means trusting in the Lord always.

Chapter Seven

FAITH-IN-ACTION PRAYERS

Faith-in-Action Prayer

Dear Jesus,

My steps are ordered by you. You have placed me in this matter, and I will glorify you because your hand is upon me.

I admit that I am challenged in understanding why you chose me in this matter, this season, this time, and this moment. My direction was going in a good way as wonderful things were happening, wonderful results in your glory, so I am suffering with thoughts about why you would allow this unseen event to occur.

I denounce any attempt to override your glory. I am hurting, but not forsaken. I am wondering, but I am chosen. I am seeking, but I am not lost.

This is the faith you have given me to work out. This is the faith you have entrusted me to execute. Yes Lord, this is the faith you want in action.

I surrender my will to you.

I surrender my thoughts to you.

I surrender all to you.

Bless this faith, my faith into action.

In Jesus' Name,

Amen

FAITH IN ACTION

Faith-in-Action Community Prayer

Dear Jesus,

This community needs saving.

The streets are filled with despair and hopelessness. Your eyes see the degradation, the injustice, the disparity and dysfunction of all types, which is giving community members more reason to remain hopeless.

I know your call of faith is in me, Lord. I cannot allow my faith to dry up because you have put me here to do something. You said faith without works is dead. Well, I refuse to allow my faith to die while watching this community slip away. Since you have placed me here, use me in your capacity.

Oh Lord,

Bring *redemption* into this community.

Bring *peace* into this community.

Bring *hope* into this community.

Bring *justice* into this community.

Bring *salvation* into this community.

Oh Lord, rebuke the trauma, rebuke the pain, rebuke the violence, rebuke injustices and give me the faith to step out and fulfill your call in your name.

In Jesus' name,

Amen

RICHARD D. HOWELL, JR.

Faith-in-Action Gideon Prayer

Dear Jesus,

Glory to your name!

Oppressors have made me feel inadequate to put faith into action. I am in fear, I am in hiding, I am running, and I am shut down. I feel like giving up. Yes Lord, I am overwhelmed and disquieted. Even my thoughts feel hijacked and victimized.

Give me your strength.

Give me your energy.

Give me your joy.

Give me your comfort.

Give me your fire.

Reset me for your glory that I will be able to stand in your name and make my faith in you full of action, that I shall not quit, I shall come out of hiding, I shall stop running, and I shall stand and face my oppressors without doubt.

Yes, Lord Jesus, I confess my inadequacy to you, but affirm my faith in you, that what I am about to do in the face of oppression will bring out your glory world without end.

In Jesus' name,

Amen

FAITH IN ACTION

Family-in-Action Family Prayer

Dear Jesus,

This family is your family. We are your family. You are head of this home. We submit to you and only you.

Bless this family, oh Lord, to produce and manifest your purpose today. All that we have comes from you, and all that we shall be is because of you. Teach us to be content with what we have, and make our love grow for each other in this family.

As you love us, may we love each other.

As you forgive us, may we forgive each other.

As you redeemed us, may we redeem each other.

Put our faith into action that we will endure all matters with our family, that we will trust in you, hope in you, and have confidence in you.

Yes Lord Jesus, this family and home are yours. Do your will with us so that we may live out your glory.

In Jesus' name,

Amen

Faith-in-Action Prayer for a Loved One

Dear Jesus,

Remember (insert name) who is overwhelmed with these challenges.

I intercede and stand in this gap for (insert name) whose faith is challenged and needs your help. This is the right time to call on your name. Your ears are not too heavy to hear. Your hand is not short to save. If you don't hear, who shall? If you don't save, who will?

Lord, return your power to (insert name).

In Jesus' name,

Amen

FAITH-IN-ACTION STORIES

The following faith stories are inspiring real-life accounts from three Christians who shared with me what their faith in action means to them. Each story has something powerful to teach us about God's love, mercy, and His unyielding presence in our lives. As you read each story, prepare a space for the Holy Spirit to speak to you about your own faith in action. Know that every story, yours and mine included, is unique. God's plan for our lives is also unique. I thank God for the stories like the ones you are about to read because they remind us of how important it is to understand that God's hand is on each of us.

We always thank God for all of you and continually mention you in our prayers.

We remember before our God and Father your work produced by faith,

your labor prompted by love, and your endurance inspired by hope in our Lord Jesus Christ.

—THESSALONIANS 1:2-3

RICHARD D. HOWELL, JR.

AMBER'S STORY
"It rains on the just and the unjust."

I've been tested in my faith every time I had a medical issue. The first time I broke my neck and my spine, I did not know they were broken. I was walking around for months with a broken neck. When I found out, it was almost unbelievable that the Lord had allowed me to walk around with a broken neck.

The second time I broke my neck and spine, it was broken all the way down to my seventh vertebrae. I was pushed by a co-worker—just a simple push. I instantly knew there was something wrong with me because I couldn't speak. Proverbs 3:5–6 tells us to lean on Him and not on our own understanding. Usually, people don't live with a broken neck, let alone a broken spine.

I died on the operating table, but I came back. I was told I would never be able to walk again, and that I would need a tube down my throat to even sound out words. But I continued to trust in God.

> Psalms 23 tells us that we shall not want for anything. And what I wanted was to walk again and to talk again. It took me a year to learn how to speak again.

And when they brought me the wheelchair, I refused to get in. I knew that if He gave me back my voice, He would do the same for my legs.

In September 2013, I had a stroke. I drove myself to the doctor not knowing what was wrong. When he saw my face was altered, and my speech was slurred, he called an ambulance. Then in the ambulance, I had another stroke.

I was raised in a church, so I knew that fear was of the Enemy. I knew my thoughts had to be positive thoughts. My thoughts had to be spiritual thoughts. My thoughts needed to be thoughts of elevation with Christ. That very next day, I was talking to God, as I always do.

He told me, "You can get up if you want to. You don't have to call the nurse. I want you to trust me."

When the Holy Ghost speaks, if you're a believer, you do what the Holy Ghost tells you to do—so I got out of the bed and went to the bathroom. I saw that my face was untwisted.

The Enemy kept talking to me, telling me, "I didn't get you now, but I'll get you later." I kept denouncing the thoughts. I have no room for Satan in my life; I belong to God. Thirty days later, I had another stroke. I could hear the enemy in one ear saying, "I told you; I'm going to get you." And the Holy Ghost was in the other ear saying, "Get up and go dial 911."

I don't know what happened, but the next thing I remember was being in my living room with firefighters at the door. When they found me, I was pleading the blood of Jesus. And all through the ambulance ride, I was still pleading the blood of Jesus. I remember paramedics asking one another, "What is she saying?" I heard one reply, "She's pleading the blood of Jesus."

God did not give us fear, but the spirit of a sound mind.

> *Things are not how I thought they should be, but I know it rains on the just and the unjust. This is why we should keep the faith. We must remember that this too shall pass.*

As it says in Proverbs 3, when we lie down, our sleep should be sweet.

Faith takes courage. As African-American women we need to be delivered and that takes courage, strength, and trust. You cannot be ashamed or worried about what people are going to say. Yet, we walk in fear, never uttering anything to anybody. I'm walking through a storm right now. However, many of the storms are not mine, but have been laid in my lap through family members.

A year ago, my daughter left her kids with my boyfriend, and said she'd be back. It turned out that I had to raise those kids on my own. In the process I learned that we have to learn to forgive each other. Sometimes we wouldn't hear from my daughter in months. But, recently she showed up two days before my birthday.

> *When it comes to faith, it's you and God.*

Despite everything, God is blessing me. While we are in the middle of a storm, God is yet blessing me. I can still help my daughter with a car, and with an apartment. You can help people, but in reality, you can only help those who want to help themselves. But, that's where prayer comes in. Although things are not often how we think they should be, remember that "It rains on the just and the unjust." I have my own needs, but I'm not going to be selfish. I'm going to keep the faith and trust God. This too shall pass.

RICHARD D. HOWELL, JR.

VALERIE'S STORY
Faith is Eternal

I always thank my God as I remember you in my prayers because I hear about your love for all his holy people and your faith in the Lord Jesus.

- PHILEMON 1:4-5

I always had belief in God. It was never a question for me. Faith was always there. Believing in who God was came before the faith. At the age of four, my cousins and I were playing house. Somehow we got separated, and I ended up in the bedroom in bed with my great-uncle. He lived with us in a big old white house way out in the sticks. He started doing something to me, but I didn't understand it at the time. My mother came up the stairs and into the room.

"What are you doing?" she yelled, and kicked him out of the house. From that point forward, I felt that I was the one doing something wrong. Also, my mother and I had an estranged relationship. At the time she was in a relationship with my younger brother's dad.

At age five, I took ownership over helping my mother with my siblings. My mother worked nights in St. Paul, and she decided to take the kids to have my brother's dad watch us while she worked. I became the caretaker even though I was the middle child of five siblings because I was the biggest and the tallest.

FAITH IN ACTION

My brother's dad would wake us up—I was first, then my sister, and then my brother. We'd go to the bathroom, and that's when it started. He made me stand on the toilet and then abused me sexually. This went on for a long time. At my age, I didn't understand—but already I believed in God. I knew God was love and good, and that the opposite of that was the devil.

The abuse went on for a long time. But he'd always say, "Don't do anything, don't say anything." It was my brother's dad.

Finally, I got a vaginal infection, so my mother took me to the doctor where they inserted medication into me.

I was always a bigger kid for my age. I would walk slumped over because I didn't want people to look at me. I kept my head down and would fantasize all the time; I was always out-of-body, trying to escape what was happening. I started using heroin at fifteen. When I was young, my neighbor was always looking at me. I know what those looks mean now. He stopped me one day and said, "I'll give you some money to buy lunch."

"Okay," I said. He would take me to school, but before he let me get out, he would fondle me. I had talked myself into thinking that was fine, and I might as well get something for it.

But as soon as I accepted the Lord, just like that, it was over. Total deliverance. I still had low self-esteem, and I still had anger. Those emotions are with me to this day. But, God started revealing things to me in a different way. People had given up on me, but the Lord took all that and turned it around. Eventually, I was able to start ministering. And then the Holy Ghost told me to tell my story.

"Absolutely not," I said.

Then we had a dialogue. Eventually, I was convinced. And so I've been sharing my story. I've shared *everything*. I tell people, "There's hope. The same God that delivered me will deliver you."

People told me I couldn't go back to school, but I went back and got my GED. And then I went back and received my bachelor's. Then I got my graduate degree. My first job was in family and children's services as a social worker. I've worked in courts advocating for women. I've been able to give back, which has empowered me.

The same God that did it for me, He'll do it for you. Now, I'm sixty-four. I'm going to live to twice that. There's nothing in my bones and nothing in my body that tells me to stop.

> *Faith in action is the substance of things hoped for, and evidence of things not seen. So, I cannot give up on Him. Faith is eternal.*

The race is not given to the swift or the strong, but to those who endure to the end.

My faith was most recently tested with my son. I had been talking to him about his eating habits and about improving his diet. One Wednesday night, I received a call that my son was in the hospital. I believed in my spirit that God was going to do something. My son's operation was successful, and although I wanted it to be done, I could sense something telling me, "We're not done." Then I got a call, and we had to rush him to the hospital. He's a young man, but had to get a triple bypass, and his odds of living were not good.

I had some doubt. His heart was going too fast. They had to reduce his heart rate. My faith was tested, but then everyone

FAITH IN ACTION

left the room, and it was only God, my son, and me. My son was unconscious, and you could see his pulse on the monitor. I began to pray and intercede on his behalf. I believed that with his faith and my faith, even though he was unconscious I should pray. As I started speaking in tongues, the monitor started going down. I said, "Lord, we have to stabilize him." Then I remembered that the testing of faith is eternal.

After it was all over, my son said he saw me speaking in tongues and praying. He said, "I wasn't afraid. I believe God. The Lord told me I would not die that day." I believed God, and while we were going through that, I still had the faith to believe. Without faith in action, my son would have died.

> *So for me, faith is not giving up. Never will I give up on God. Because I have experienced those tests, the faith that I now have has made me much stronger.*

In the end, tests are not bad. In fact, it ends up where we can relate those messages to each other. It always comes back to encouraging each other. Pain is good. It's a warning sign. If you're going through pain and trials, faith and perseverance will never leave nor forsake you. And that is God.

Faith is just God. Period. For me, my entire life, I asked God for everything. My self-esteem is still guttering. But I know to stand anyway because He tells me to stand. I can't see anything. I know what I need and want, but I can't see that. I have to ask Him, "What should I wear?" I don't want to be judged.

RICHARD D. HOWELL, JR.

> *Faith is knowing nothing, but trusting in Him for everything.*

God has a real sense of humor. Today, I minister better to men than I do to women although men are the ones that have hurt me. But I have to remember that at some point something happened to them. The reason they keep doing things to their wives and children is that something happened to them. They don't understand that they can be vulnerable. They have this mask, and they're walking around trying to uphold what a man is supposed to be. But inside, they're five and six years old. God continues to give me these messages. I have a notebook thick with the messages God has made me write down.

So that you may know the certainty of the things you have been taught.

- LUKE 1:4

> *Faith—I can't see it, but I don't have to worry about it.*

To me, God is faith. I have had to depend on Him, so He is my faith. Everything that happened to me, I've always kept a

FAITH IN ACTION

channel with God. My faith is tested every single day. I function on God. He's been my faith, my substance, my everything. I can't function without Him.

Do you really believe God, or do you believe in Him for the rewards? When I was a little girl, I had a dream that God and the Devil were fighting over my soul. When I woke up screaming, I looked out the window and saw two red eyes smiling at me.

God has gotten me out of every situation. My faith, to me, is God. I don't know how else to describe faith. If you trust Him, there's your faith right there. The relationship you have with God is your faith.

I believe God says to us, "I am the shield that says faith to you on it."

Therefore I tell you, whatever you ask for in prayer, believe that you have received it, and it will be yours.

— MARK 11:24

RICHARD D. HOWELL, JR.

RITA'S STORY:
God said, "Say it Again."

It started when I was a kid. I don't remember my age because I think God erased some of the little details. I wasn't ten. My father's business partner was going to pick up something, and I rode along with him to his house. He told me to lie on the floor, and next thing I know my pants were down. He was a big guy, probably three hundred pounds, and I was a little kid and I couldn't fight him.

He didn't take my virginity, but he sodomized me. He put his hands over my mouth. I had heard in church that God was a protector, so I called out, "Why, God? Why are you letting this happen?"

But I still couldn't get him off me. He finished doing his business. He told me not to tell anyone; otherwise, he'd kill my entire family. I believed him. From that day, people asked what was wrong with me. I began to act out as a kid. I didn't bother with people, and stayed within myself. I didn't talk to God. I didn't talk to anybody. I didn't trust my father or my mother. I didn't trust because nobody protected me.

As a teenager, I started doing drugs. I left the church and went out on my own. I was approached to do prostitution. I thought, "They take it, so why not get paid for it?" I don't remember sections of my life because of what has happened to me. But one night I remember it was raining. I had always loved the rain. To me, it has always felt like a cleanse. But on this particular night, I was done. We had been using drugs and living in chaos. I told God I'd kill myself if He didn't take me out of this.

Then a woman pulled up. She dried my clothes, fed me, and

let me sleep. When I got up, I felt better. I was ready to go back out and do what I needed to do. I forgot God. Shortly after that time, I was on the bus, and a voice said, "Look out the window." When I did I saw my old pastor in a trench coat, staring at me with his hands in his pockets. I was always one of his favorites back when I went to church. Every time I heard voices telling me to do something right, I'd always thought it was his voice. When I "saw him" from inside the bus, my pastor had already passed away, but his voice still told me to go to church, so I did.

Then Jesus said, "Did I not tell you that if you believe, you will see the glory of God?"

- JOHN 11:40

God started talking to me. I said, "If that's true, I want to know all He has for me." I went to church that Sunday, and when they did the altar call, I catapulted out of my seat and they took me to the back.

Shortly thereafter, I went to visit my mother out of town and we went to church that Sunday. When I came out of that church, I didn't know who I was. I felt new. Everything looked like a kaleidoscope. I could see things differently and clearly. The snow, the trees, my momma, everything looked different to me. Everything was brand new to me. That was the ultimate. After that, I could always see God. He was always present to me.

RICHARD D. HOWELL, JR.

> *I can see Him standing in the mirror behind me. I hear Him talking to me. That's the God I know. He talks to me like I'm talking to you now.*

I never told anyone my story. I didn't know who I was, and I didn't know how to act, how to respond to anybody, or how to have a friend. I had my first son because I needed something for myself, and then I had four more children. I never wanted people to babysit my kids, so I always made sure I was around. I opened a daycare because I didn't want to leave my kids with anybody. I remember working third shift to get through school, and my son would babysit. I was very protective over my children.

But when you ask, you must believe and not doubt, because the one who doubts is like a wave of the sea, blown and tossed by the wind.

- JAMES 1:6

But then I got married, and my husband molested my daughter for over two years. Now looking back, I see there were signs, but at the time I didn't know. She would run away. She was using drugs. When I found out, I called the church. I wanted to kill him…I was fixin' to kill him, but God told me to call the Bishop.

FAITH IN ACTION

So I called the church and asked to speak to Bishop. He was in a meeting, and the assistant asked me if it was important.

"Well, I'm about to go kill somebody. You ask Bishop if that's important." Then I explained to him what happened.

Bishop said, "Don't say anything to him. Act normal, and come into the office tomorrow."

I really wanted to hurt the Bishop right then. He wanted me to stay with the enemy for twenty-four hours and pretend I didn't want to take the closest knife and kill him. Of course, he wanted to have sex that night, which really tested my faith. But God kept saying, "Don't say nothing. Don't do nothing." So I went along with it.

I had no pain because God said, "Don't worry about it." I could literally feel God's arms around me when I wanted to kill my husband.

> *Ever since I got the Holy Ghost, I could never not feel God. So there was never a reason to doubt Him. He always speaks to me. He's always held me.*

I knew something had to come out of this. The way He made me feel, and the peace He gave me—but I still had my anger. And then another big test happened when I felt like my family abandoned me. My sister came over to visit one day and began to tell me I didn't deserve my kids and that I was an unfit mother. I heard her out and then quietly told her, "I love you." Then, I let her go. After the door closed behind her, I felt angry.

At that moment, God told me to recite Proverbs 3:5. After I read the verse out loud, God said, "Say it again." He kept repeating His instructions, so I kept reciting the verse, and then He'd tell me to say it again. I felt Him. He grabbed me. I began jumping and screaming so hard that I fractured my feet.

All that happened, and I kept getting people looking at me and talking about me. Still today, it's hard for me to trust people. I've experienced so much depression in my life. I've gone through stuff that nobody knows about.

Whenever I feel paralyzed, I hear God's voice commanding, "Say it again." No matter what you're going through, listen to God.

Trust in the LORD with all your heart and lean not on your own understanding; in all your ways submit to him, and he will make your paths straight.

—PROVERBS 3:5

ACKNOWLEDGMENTS

To Bettye Howell, my wife and best friend for more than forty-three years who has been by my side without fail. Without her, this book could not have been written.

To Richie and Michelle, Andrea and Felix, and to my grandchildren who continue to manifest a true and spiritual family dynamic placing my faith in action.

To Josephine Howell, my mother, whose strong faith continues to amaze me after losing her marital lover of sixty-four years and yet, remaining strong in faith.

To Shiloh Temple International Ministries for your continued support and words of encouragement

To Pastor Tim Brewington of Fellowship Church of Woodbury Minnesota for his rich insight and thoughts that helped make this book a reality.

ABOUT BISHOP RICHARD D. HOWELL, JR.

Bishop Richard D. Howell, Jr. has been the pastor of Shiloh Temple International Ministries since 1984, the same church his grandparents Reverend Howard and Sister Mattie Smith founded in Minneapolis in 1931. From his youth, he has served in just about every capacity in ministry on the local level, as the call of God was in his life to serve in the ministry years before his pastorate.

Bishop Howell holds a Bachelor's Degree in Pastoral Studies from North Central Bible College in Minneapolis, and a Masters of Arts Degree in Counseling Psychology from St. Thomas University in St. Paul. In August 2010 he was awarded an Honorary Doctorate of Divinity from Aenon Bible College, Indianapolis, IN, he received his Doctorate of Divinity from Friends International Christian University in 2005, and was awarded an Honorary Doctorate of Divinity from St. Thomas College, Jackson, Florida in 2003.

Bishop Howell recently accepted a position on the Board of Regents with St. Thomas College, Minneapolis, MN; he also received an Honorary Doctorate of Divinity October 19, 2013, from St. Thomas College, Minneapolis, MN.

Bishop Howell has worked in management for the government and Job Corps of America in St. Paul, MN.

He has received several awards and appreciation recognizing his work in the community including an appreciation from The National Institute on Media and the Family; and the 2000 Recognition and Appreciation Award for his contribution to education to the State of Minnesota by the James Meredith Institute. He was also featured in a Pastoral Recognition article in *Upscale* Magazine, for the Affluent Lifestyle in 2000; and an award in recognition of his dedication and leadership in service to justice in Hennepin County from the Hennepin County Attorney's Office. Bishop Howell is currently on the Hennepin County Sheriff's Advisory Board and the Minneapolis Urban League Board.

Bishop Howell is the Diocesan over the 7th Episcopal District of the Pentecostal Assemblies of the World, Inc., which is the Minnesota, Wisconsin, Dakotas District Council (MWDDC), and the diocese in which he has served as District Superintendent, District Youth President, General Body Council Chairman, District Elder, and Suffragan Bishop. He currently serves on the Executive Board of the Pentecostal Assemblies of the World, Inc.

He is the author of *Possessors of the Kingdom* which was published in 2008.